KIDS THROUGHOUT HISTORY™

Kids During the Time of the Maya

Caroline M. Levchuck

The Rosen Publishing Group's
PowerKids Press™
New York

For Peggy and Richie . . . a couple of crazy kids from the Bronx.
And very special thanks to Barbara and Justin Kerr.

Published in 1999 by The Rosen Publishing Group, Inc.
29 East 21st Street, New York, NY 10010

First Edition

Book Design: Danielle Primiceri

Photo Credits: Cover and pp. 11, 12 © Justin Kerr; p. 4 © Erich Lessing/Art Resource, (inset) © Buddy Mays/International Stock; p. 7 © Buddy Mays/International Stock, (inset) Andromedia Interactive Ltd.; p. 8 © Greg Johnston/International Stock, (inset) © Anako; p. 15 © Elizabeth Simpson, (inset) © Justin Kerr; p. 16 © Dr. Kurt Stravenhagen Collection/Art Resource, (inset) © Anako; p. 19 Courtesy of Zona Arqueológica de Chichen-Itzá; p. 20 © Buddy Mays/International Stock.

Levchuck, Caroline M.
    Kids in the time of the Maya / Caroline M. Levchuck.
       p.   cm. — (Kids throughout history)
    Includes index.
    Summary: Discusses the food, dress, schooling, games, housing, and culture of children in the ancient Mayan civilization.
    ISBN 0-8239-5258-4
    1. Maya children—Juvenile literature. 2. Mayas—Social life and customs—Juvenile literature.
    [1. Mayas—Social life and customs.] I. Title. II. Series.
    F1435.3.C47W76 1998
    305.23'097281'0901—dc21
                                       97-49265
                                          CIP
                                          AC

Manufactured in the United States of America

Contents

The Maya

The Mayan people of thousands of years ago made up one of the most important ancient **civilizations** (SIH-vih-lih-ZAY-shunz) in the Americas. The Maya lived in parts of what we now call Central America and Mexico. They were religious people. The Maya were known for their skills as artists, farmers, **mathematicians** (MATH-muh-TIH-shunz), and city builders. The ancient Maya were able to build huge **pyramids** (PEER-uh-midz) without the help of wheels or metal tools. They were most powerful between about 250 and 900 AD.

The ancient Mayan civilization and its pyramids, such as this one at Chichen Itza, Mexico, go back to the year 2000 BC. Mayans still live there today.

A Mayan City

The ancient Mayan civilization was made up of cities. Many cities were connected to others by wide paved roads that were used to trade goods with other cities. The trade of food and a stone called jade was important to Mayan city life. Mayan cities had **temples** (TEM-pulz) and markets where people bought and sold goods. Wealthy families lived close to the center of these cities. But many children, including a boy named Seven Ahaw, lived with their families on farms just outside the city.

These are the ruins of the ancient Mayan city of Uxmal in what is now the Yucatan Peninsula of Mexico.

UNITED STATES

GULF OF
MEXICO

Florida

CUBA

MEXICO

Yucatan

GUATEMALA

CARIBBEAN
SEA

PANAMA

PACIFIC
OCEAN

Growing Up Maya

Like most Mayan children, Seven Ahaw got his name from the Mayan calendar. He was born on the seventh day of the month, and the name of that day was Ahaw. Ahaw is like a day of the week. Seven lived with his family near the southern city of Tikal.

Seven's father was a farmer, so he and his family needed to live close to their fields. Their home was an oval hut. The walls were made of strong, thin poles that were **thatched** (THACHT) together with grasses. A woven grass roof kept out the rain.

◀ *Though Mayans no longer live in the ancient cities, such as Tikal, there are many Mayan villages that still exist today.*

Religion

The Maya believed in beings greater than humans called gods. All Mayan gods were related to nature. For example, there was a sun god, a moon god, and a corn god. The powerful Mayan **priests** (PREESTS) made offerings to the gods at great temples built on top of tall pyramids. Seven and his family would take part in **festivals** (FES-tih-vulz) honoring the gods by watching a **sacred** (SAY-kred) ball game. It was played on a large grass court. This game was a little like soccer and basketball combined.

This painting is from a Mayan vase that dates back to about 800 AD. It shows two men in costume playing the sacred ball game. ▶

Food

Maize (MAYZ), or corn, was the most important part of the ancient Mayan diet. Each morning, Seven's mother made **tortillas** (tor-TEE-yahz). She ground the maize into a thick dough on a **metate** (may-TAH-tay). Then she made thin cakes and cooked them on a stone griddle over a fire. Seven and his friends would come in from the fields to find warm tortillas topped with honey waiting for them. The Maya also enjoyed tortillas stuffed with beans or meat.

This painting is on an ancient Mayan pot from between 750 and 900 AD. It shows a woman making tortillas on her metate.

Farming

Seven and his father planted maize on their farm. They planted bean seeds next to the maize. As the bean vines grew, they wrapped around the maize plants and supported them. The Maya believed that this support, together with pulling weeds every day, would keep the maize god happy. Then they would have a good crop. When the crop was good, Seven's father shared his food with families who didn't farm. Men who didn't farm did other work, such as helping to build pyramids and other buildings.

The Maya called the maize god "Hun Hun Ahaw," which means "first lord." ▶

Weaving

The making of fine cloth was important work for the ancient Maya. Seven's mother, like other Mayan women, **spun** (SPUN) and wove cloth from cotton and wool. Seven's mother would strap a **loom** (LOOM) around her lower back like a belt and weave cloth. She taught her daughters how to weave clothing and blankets for their family. They wove plain skirts for themselves. For Seven and their father, the girls wove cloths that the men wore around their waists. They also made fancy, dyed cloth for wealthy Mayans to buy.

◄ *This ancient sculpture shows how the Maya weaved long ago. This is the same way traditional Mayan weaving is done today.*

Learning

Seven, and other farmers' kids like him, did not go to school. Only priests and the children of wealthy people were able to study and go to school. Those who went to school learned the Mayan writing system called **hieroglyphs** (HY-roh-glifs). The Maya were the only civilization to have a writing system at this time. Wealthy children also learned mathematics. The Maya were the first **culture** (KUL-cher) to have a written **symbol** (SIM-bul)—zero—that stood for nothing.

Time was very important to the Maya. In fact, they made calendars that some believe are more exact than the ones we use today. This picture shows one day ▶ *of a Mayan calendar.*

Rain Forests

The Maya found many of their **resources** (REE-sor-sez) in the **rain forests** (RAYN FOR-ests) near their land. Jade and bamboo were found in the forests. But as the Mayan people grew in number, there were fewer and fewer resources left in the rain forests. With few resources left, the Maya had no goods to trade or food to eat. By 900 AD many Maya had left the cities. They moved to other parts of Central America where they could find new land for farming.

◄ *Many Mayan ruins, such as these at Tikal, have been discovered deep in the rain forest.*

21

Forever Maya

By the year 1450, there were very few Maya left in the ancient cities. When the Spanish explorers came to the Americas in the 1500s, they easily took over Mayan lands. But luckily, some of the Maya survived. Today, there are many relatives of the ancient Maya living in Mexico and Guatemala. They are still known for their fine weaving and delicious tortillas. Mayan children keep their culture alive by learning and practicing many of the ways of the ancient Maya.

Glossary

civilization (SIH-vih-lih-ZAY-shun) A group of people living in an organized and similar way.

culture (KUL-cher) The beliefs, customs, art, and religion of a people.

festival (FES-tih-vul) A day or special time of recognizing someone or something important.

hieroglyphs (HY-roh-glifs) A form of writing that uses pictures for different words or sounds.

loom (LOOM) A tool used to make fabric.

maize (MAYZ) Corn.

mathematician (MATH-muh-TIH-shun) A person who studies math.

metate (may-TAH-tay) A stone on which corn was ground.

priest (PREEST) A religious leader.

pyramid (PEER-uh-mid) A large structure with a square bottom and triangular sides.

rain forest (RAYN FOR-est) A very wet area that has many kinds of plants, trees, and animals.

resource (REE-sors) Something in nature that is bought and sold.

sacred (SAY-kred) Something that is highly respected.

spin (SPIN) To draw out and twist cotton into thread.

symbol (SIM-bul) Something that stands for something else.

temple (TEM-pul) A place of worship.

thatched (THACHT) When something is covered with dried straw or grass and woven into thick sheets.

tortilla (tor-TEE-yah) A flat bread made from corn or flour.

Index